I0441716

Endorsements

Titania's life's journey and path to faith will be an inspiration for all who read about her "modern day miracle." --Thomas J. Pernice, father, entrepreneur, and former senior White House official in the Reagan and Bush Administrations.

"Jesus Appeared" is a powerful and colorful account of how one woman's spiritual journey through a sequence of miracles can offer faith and inspiration to anyone searching for love, hope and the meaning of life." --Liza Utter, TV host, author and founder / President of Life's A Party, Inc. and www.lizaamericashost.com

"Beautifully written from a place of healing...'Jesus Appeared' is a powerful, redemptive story of one woman's miraculous and life-changing encounter."--Mark White, Worship Pastor; Calvary Community Church.

"Titania's journey to Jesus gives rise to the hope of God's promise and the comfort of knowing Christ is present in all of our lives."--Bill Armour, CEO Burke Williams, Inc. / www.burkewilliamsspa.com

"A moving masterpiece of beautifully written words, describing a past of turmoil to literally touching the heavens."--Dr Raymond Hall, D.C.; PILLO1 inventor and Sports Medicine Chiropractor.

"For a hurting soul searching for peace, this story will ignite your faith and restore your hope. Her story reveals in such a touching way that God is always with us, and working in our lives even when we don't recognize or acknowledge his presence."—Zina Bell, Sr. National Account Executive at Salem Communications.

"A story with honesty and candor that is refreshing and at times sobering... this inspiring read is a reminder that miracles come in many forms and happen when you least expect them." –Ragnar Rosinkranz, Composer and Music Producer / www.ragnarmusic.com

JESUS APPEARED

A
Modern-Day
Miracle

Titania M. Lindfors and Laura J. Adams

WESTBOW
P R E S S
A DIVISION OF THOMAS NELSON

WestBow Press books may be ordered through booksellers or by contacting:

WestBow Press
A Division of Thomas Nelson
1663 Liberty Drive
Bloomington, IN 47403
www.westbowpress.com
1 (866) 928-1240

ISBN: 978-1-4908-1718-7 (sc)
ISBN: 978-1-4908-1717-0 (e)

Library of Congress Control Number: 2013921626

Printed in the United States of America.

WestBow Press rev. date: 12/10/2013

Contents

In loving memory of my dear cousins,

Jeanette and Agnetha

Introduction

At the age of twenty-three, I had a supernatural experience with the Lord Jesus Christ that dramatically changed my life. Ever since that very special day, I've had the opportunity to share the miracle with many people in their time of need. I hope this may be an encouragement to you as well.

This is my story.

Fatherless in America

My mother, a classic Nordic beauty, grew up with several siblings in a small historical Swedish village. Her parents were hardworking and poor like most of the villagers who struggled to survive in harsh conditions. As she blossomed into a young adult it was difficult for her to find purpose there. At eighteen years old she made the courageous decision to leave her family and familiar homeland for America on the quest for a better life.

My idealistic mother envisioned her future abroad with sincere optimism, like a clear open road leading to immeasurable opportunity. Her overseas travel led her to Los Angeles, California— the destination of her unrealized potential. It was the spring of 1957. "Around The World In 80 Days" won the Academy Award for Best Picture, the final episode of "I Love Lucy" aired on CBS Television, and the Brooklyn Dodgers' move from New York to their new Los Angeles home was approved by the National League owners. The atmosphere of hope in the West mesmerized her.

It was there, soon after she arrived, that my mother met my charismatic biological father. Culturally he was different than men she had known in Sweden and his unique carefree qualities intrigued her. Falling in love with an American was not something she had planned. Dating him led her down a path of unexpected life turns when she became pregnant with me out of wedlock a few years into their relationship. As her pregnancy progressed, my mother was disheartened because my father began to withdraw from their relationship. Her effort to create a stable life was shattered when he left her to raise me alone. He visited us a few times when I was a newborn and then he simply disappeared. I saw him only once when I was nineteen.

By twenty-one years of age, my mother was a single parent living in a foreign country without financial assistance or family support. It wasn't the future she hoped for when she left Sweden, but she loved me very much and summoned the fortitude to persevere through her unchartered life challenges. She eventually secured a full-time hostess job at the landmark Du-par's restaurant at the Farmer's Market near Fairfax and 3rd Street in Los Angeles. The nine-seat counter café was bustling with locals and Hollywood celebrities whose chronic patronage was inspired by their famous hotcake breakfasts and scratch-made cherry pies that lined wall mounted glass shelves. Business was booming to keep her busy, yet her minimum wage salary was insufficient. The price of bread was just twenty-two cents a loaf, but our Hollywood studio apartment was often bare of the adequate nutrition and supplies a growing toddler needed.

My mother continued to navigate single parenthood with steadfast conviction that our circumstances would improve. Lacking money for a preschool expense, her only option was to rely on the kindness of strangers for my care. There was a nice couple living nearby who expressed compassion for us. As the first sign of mercy in our lives, they graciously provided me childcare for several consecutive days without requiring payment so my mother could keep her job. While they gave me some comfort in her absence, they were unfamiliar to me. I didn't have a father's hand to guide me, or friends to play with, and I was lonely without my mother.

Småland

In 1963, a few months before President John F. Kennedy was assassinated, my mother's older brother came to visit us. Uncle Hasse Lindfors was a handsome, charming man, who had traveled from Sweden to Hollywood with a mission, to encourage my mother towards an opportunity for us to thrive. He earnestly persuaded my mother to return home to Sweden by offering her a career at his furniture distribution company. She accepted his considerate offer because it was the fresh start we desperately needed.

It didn't take long for my mother to quit her job, pack up our scarce belongings, load us into her old Cadillac, and say goodbye to southern California. I was three years old when she ventured out with me on an ambitious cross-country road trip to New York where we departed for Europe on an ocean liner. My mother left America behind with renewed hope for a bountiful destiny as we embarked on the arduous two-week Trans-Atlantic crossing towards our new beginning.

We moved to the southern Provence of Småland *('Small lands')*, where the founder of Ikea, Ingvar Kamprad, was raised. The region is particularly lush with dark green forests, many cool lakes, and stunning reserves boasting vast wildlife.

We stayed with my Uncle Hasse, Aunt UllaBritt, and four cousins—Lotta, Agnetha, Jeanette, and Johan, until we were able to secure an apartment. They made me feel welcome in their respite for hospitality country home that was surrounded by a sprawling open yard bordering the forest edge and water channels leading to the town harbor.

My cousins were impressed by my American heritage. When we first met, they made a sincere effort to speak both English and Swedish with me. "Want to play with us? *"Vill du leka med oss?"* I surprised them by responding in Swedish, *Ja jatte garna!"* ("Yes, I really do!"), since my mother had been teaching me bilingually. The five of us became instant friends. We found inventive ways to create amusement by playing in the forest, 'snow skiing' on my Aunt's family room carpet, and battling pillow fights in the garden. But our favorite game starter was Uncle Hasse's weed eating goat. He lived in the yard tied by a rope to a pole that kept him from running away, but didn't stop him from chasing us when we came near. Sometimes we'd have to climb up a tree to stay clear of his aggressive prodding horns. We'd screech nervously—wondering who would be the one caught by the grumpy whiskered goat that we grew to cherish. Laughter filled my days that first summer in Sweden. I began to feel like I was 'home'.

Midsummer Dream

My mother found us a tiny rural apartment where we shared one bedroom in the town of Tranås, near Lake Sommen, one of the largest clear-water lakes in Sweden, with more that 360 islands to explore. There were very few children to play with near our side of town, so I spent most of my young life fascinated with nature. Inspired by the Fairy Queen character in Shakespeare's "A Midsummer's Nights Dream", my mother had appropriately named me 'Titania', since we lived in a tranquil haven that offered the perfect backdrop for an idyllic childhood. Playing in the woods among clustered tall trees, enjoying lakeside picnics my mother had prepared for us, jumping from a trampoline off the deck into the water for daily lake swims, and riding lessons at the local horse stable filled my summer recess. Cross-country skiing, outdoor ice-skating, and snow angel creating became my joy filled recreation on our short Scandinavian winter days where the moon lit up our snow banks.

My life was peaceful, but I held an incessant feeling that I was *different*. My mother was good to me and did her best as a single parent to raise me to flourish, but I always felt alone in my serene surroundings, suffering a desire for family that could not be fulfilled solely by her. The loneliness I felt in America when I was away from my mother resurfaced in Sweden like a vice grip that began to pinch my heart.

Seeking Normal

After living a year in our first Tranås apartment, my mother moved us closer to the center of town to an area where I could meet more children. That's where I met Susanne. We were both five years old and she befriended me quickly. I liked her simply because she liked me. She was the first friend I'd met apart from cousins, however our relationship was short lived after she enticed me to do something my mother wished she hadn't. While we were shopping at the main street market, Suzanne convinced me to steal money from my mother's wallet so we could buy candy. We were abruptly intercepted when my mother spotted us in line at the kiosk attempting to make a purchase with money she knew couldn't have been ours. She didn't correct me publicly, but she gave me a stern reprimand when we returned home. That was the last time I was given permission to play with Suzanne. I heartily lamented such a quick found and lost first friend.

Uncle Hasse often required my mother to travel on extended business trips to Germany and England. My Aunt Ullabritt took care of me occasionally, but my mother hired an elderly couple to become my full time day-care providers until the age of seven. I spent most of my days with bright-eyed Eva and kind-hearted Gosta who became like surrogate grandparents to me. The loving environment they had created provided me a sense of stability while my mother was gone. Their quaint home and tiny backyard was a place of comfort that felt like I was covered by a warm down blanket whenever I stayed there.

Several of the neighborhood children hosted summer bike races on Eva and Gosta's road. They often invited me to join but I was a little intimidated. I wasn't a typical kid compared to all of those children who were from traditional families. Living with a single mother, I was a fatherless American girl who was seeking normal—wishing for the family lives they all had. Though I did my best to win, I was unable to keep up with the other racers on my single speed tricycle that my mother had bought for me.

Once I was enrolled as an elementary school first grader, my season with my day care parents ended. I was heartbroken when I had to say goodbye for the last time to Eva and Gosta, who I'd grown to love and who loved me unconditionally in return.

Everything in my young life kept changing. The transition to the next season was a difficult one. When my mother had to leave town for work during the two summers that followed first grade, I stayed on a farm in a customary Day care home about three hours from Tranas. It was traumatic staying so far away from home and everyone who'd become familiar. Like Eva and Gosta, the proprietors were an older husband and wife, but spending every day and night for weeks with that couple was quite unpalatable compared to Eva and Gosta. The man treated me fairly, but his wife was an unhappy, mean spirited woman who was difficult to live with. I did not feel safe with her.

When my mother left me to stay there, I watched through silent tears while she prepared for her long departure. As she drove her vintage Volkswagen down the road away from where I stood to say goodbye, I ran after her screaming— yelling, *"Mama, Mama! Snalla, lamnna mig inte!"* (*"Mama, don't leave me; please! Stay with me!)*. My young skinny legs couldn't run fast enough.

Chasing her was futile because she couldn't see me flailing behind her car. My flood of tears turned to a pool of pain as she drove away, unaware of my vigorous plea. That's when my battle with separation anxiety began.

Lena and Mikael

Early the next Fall my mother's income improved. She traveled less and could afford to move us into a modern apartment complex across town where I finally had the luxury of my own bedroom. The expansiveness of the complex was overwhelming. There were several long rows of four story high buildings, that each housed dozens of units, all sharing one center courtyard that functioned as the nucleus for the entire community. While I was somewhat excited to move where everything was new, I was anxious because I knew no one and the walk to school was over three kilometers. Moving to another part of town before beginning school was monumental. Fortunately there were many children to share the forty-five minute walk with, providing me the opportunity to meet several classmates who lived in my complex. Enduring school day walks together through good and bad weather, helped to improve my social life.

Lena became my new best friend. We played at her home after our walks from school together several afternoons a week. Her quiet natured mother often invited me for supper. Originally from northern Sweden, her parents spoke with a different dialect than I was accustomed to and the sound of their speech was very calming. Whenever I visited they made me feel like I was a member of their dynamic family. I relished every opportunity when the aroma of fresh baked bread served with lingonberry jam and traditional meatballs beckoned me to dine with Lena, her parents, two sisters, and older brother together around a large family table.

The pleasure of the moments I spent with Lena's family began to fade when Lena's brother, who seemed annoyed by me for a reason unknown, would tease me in school in front of other students. His aggression once caused a permanent scar when he threw a small tree branch that hit my left eye, causing it to bleed. Regardless, my intense need to keep my friendship with Lena intact was more profound than my fear of her brother's unwarranted taunting.

On my eighth birthday, Uncle Hasse gifted me with an impressive imported bicycle to ride with my group of neighborhood friends. The fashionable German Pop Cycle with a square wicker basket mounted by leather straps between the tall handlebars was my first big girl bike. No one else in my community had ever seen one quite like it. Though I was grateful for my Uncle's generosity, all I had hoped for was a generic bike similar to all the other children.

I just wanted to be like everyone else. I submerged disappointment under an ambivalent attitude to avoid revealing my insecurity to anyone—including Uncle Hasse.

As our circle of neighborhood friends grew, we gathered often to play street games such as Bur ken ('The Can'); similar to the American games 'Kick the Can' or 'Hide N Seek'. We used a tin can for home base where the designated seeker counted to ten, then searched for hiders. Whenever a hider was found, both seeker and hider raced back to home base. Whoever arrived first called out the other player's name. The game continued until the last untagged hider made it safely to home base, as the winner, and yelled *"Burken är sparkad!"* Playing a part in those competitive games increased my confidence. That's when I met Mikael.

Mikael, who was a year older than me, exuded self-assurance beyond his age through his engaging big brown eyes. He had a unique sense of humor that made me laugh and he wasn't shy about his feelings for me. Almost every day after school he'd stand by my first floor apartment balcony, a few doors down from where he lived, calling for me "Titania! Titania!"

I began to shift my devoted attention from Lena to Mikael. We spent most of our spare time together. Though we were young, our bond developed into a sweet innocent romance. I'd never had a boy treat me as special as Mikael did. He made me feel as if I was the best girl in town—loving me just for me. The season we shared enriched my life. Just being with him helped to gently release the vice grip feeling that pinched my heart.

Falling tree leaves expressed a change of weather after several months of afternoons together. Mikael's parents, who had grown fond of me, requested I sit down in their family room one afternoon so they could speak with me about something important. I looked at Mikael. He seemed calm. His father, a strong but gentle man who reminded me of a dark haired Santa Claus, was vulnerable and transparent with worry as he revealed the news, "Mikael has a brain tumor and will be going away for a while". I heard the words, but didn't know what to think or say. Their only child needed surgery to save his life. The fragility of that moment made me very sad and left an indelible impression on me.

Mikael soon left for a season that seemed indefinite. I didn't hear from him or anything about him for months, until one day he came to my apartment after recovering from his operation. I answered the door to see his shaved head wrapped up entirely with a wide white bandage. His eyes lit up as he grinned from ear to ear upon seeing my face. We hugged each other for a soothing moment, sharing the hope that everything would turn out well. Mikael fought a good fight for life but sadly he lost the battle and died nine months later.

Losing my first true love was devastating. I missed Mikael deeply without handling it too well; growing more attached to Lena with fear of losing her too. I expressed my anxiety through possessive behavior, which proved to be unhealthy for our friendship. When a new girl Kajsa moved into our apartment complex, we all played together until they nudged me aside to spend time without me. Generally I had to plead with them to allow me to join their play dates. Sometimes they were agreeable, but usually they responded "No, not today Ti-Ti".

Lena and Kajsa's exclusivity added rejection to the mix of my loneliness and separation anxiety. I had lost Mikael and it seemed I was about to lose my best girlfriend of two years. The pain of that potent combination was severe. The girl looking in from the outside of the friendship circle became my reality. I felt as if I wasn't good enough for anyone—except for my mother or cousins. *I wondered why I was 'different'? Who would be my friend? Why did I have to keep losing the people I'd grown to love?* Though I wasn't aware of God in my life, He must have heard my heartache and inspired the change that followed my loss.

Oscar

On the Christmas Eve after Mikael's death, my mother arranged for me to visit Lena. She requested I stay with her until I was called for to return home for a special Christmas gift that she had for me. Eager with anticipation, I wondered, *what it could be?* I could never have guessed correctly, when I opened the door to see my mother sitting on the kitchen floor with a huge smile on her face. In her lap she gently cuddled my tiny little surprise. As I walked towards her she lifted up to me the fulfillment of my greatest childhood wish —my own puppy!

Oscar was an eight-pound, curly haired, wide-eyed, miniature Daschund that brought immense fulfillment to my life. He immediately became *'my everything'*; bridging the loneliness gap that my losses had left me with. Oscar and I were inseparable. By sharing every day with a loyal companion, I didn't feel so alone anymore. He went places with me and did things I was certain not too many dogs had done before. He walked with me through the woods searching for squirrels, visited Uncle Hasse's office, played dress up with my many dolls, and rode in my Pop Cycle basket as we sped on two wheels through town.

The bike with the basket I was initially embarrassed to own became the very carrier my beloved Oscar needed to join me wherever I went. We became part of a Dog 'club', attended animal parties and were guests at a hamster birthday celebration.

My compliant little puppy went everywhere with me except to school— which he would have if he'd been allowed.

Once Oscar had become my best friend, my mother met a suitable man who adored her. Bo was a former member of the Swedish Army, working as a certified teacher. Their casual relationship evolved quickly to exclusive dating. When my mother decided it was time for me to meet him, I hid behind our apartment sofa as he arrived to visit. After much persuasion, my mother convinced me to come out of hiding to present myself and meet the man she was in love with. When they made the decision to marry a few years later, I didn't quite welcome Bo with open arms. His dedicated presence represented more potential loss for me. My mother and I had lived together for all of my life. I was jealous for her devoted attention. Questions pounded my thoughts. *How would my relationship with my mother be changed? What would it be like living with a man—a father in our home?*

The lifestyle adjustment for a family of two that became three was significant, yet Bo was committed to developing the father-daughter relationship I had always longed for. He was exceptionally patient. He helped me through my pained efforts to complete the math and chemistry school homework I struggled with and hated. I'd scream with frustrated angst. He'd gently calm me down while he'd offered constructive assistance. It may have taken me a while to accept Bo, but my mother's choice to marry him was the best thing that could have happened for us.

The Ants

In the province of Småland where I grew up, it was common for youth to join the Scouts. I was ten years old when it was my turn to become a member of a nature focused Scout Troop that was sponsored by Missions Church—the place where I first heard about God. The troop was divided into groups named after an animal or creature. My group became 'The Ants'. There were several children from my hometown that I attended weekly scout meetings with to play games, acquire practical life skills, and learn about God's son Jesus in small group Bible studies.

The Troop hosted two-week countryside summer camps where my beloved Oscar was given permission to join the Troop as the Camp Mascot. He enjoyed the attention so much that he preferred the companionship of our team leader Lennart and moved into his tent for the duration of camp. I didn't mind his diverted attention because I had made new friends to spend time with who accepted me.

I admired our genuine Scout leaders who created memorable life lessons for the Troop by teaching us camping skills, how to lake fish, and fireside cooking. They also guided us through Bible studies and nightly campfire songs, seamlessly integrating a Christian message that inspired faith in a relatable, good, and loving God. I left each camp more intrigued about the God of love they talked about. However, apart from those cherished experiences, pursuing faith was not an active part of my life.

Manolito

Spending time with horses helped combat my chronic loneliness. I was eleven years old, when my good friend Helena and I started riding together. As horseless equestrian lovers, we accepted every offer we were given to ride. We were ecstatic when farmers Gosta and Britt invited us to their ranch located about fifteen kilometers from Tranås. We spent entire summer days riding at their ranch and helping care for their many breeds of mares and geldings. Undeterred by weather, we always arrived prepared during winter wearing wool army coats, cozy snow boots, and knitted hats worn under our helmets to keep us warm. Hot chocolate and homemade sandwiches kept us content in our home away from home, where the scents of fresh hay, groomed horses, and weathered saddle leather filled the air.

Gosta approached me in the stable on a spring day with a glimmer in his eye. "Titania, I'll sell you your favorite little pony of mine for a reasonable sum if you'd like to purchase him." He had just offered me the potential to buy my first horse! My meager life savings combined with my mother and Bo's generous financial contribution made another wish of mine come true. Manolito was a long-maned, chubby grey and white pony, which stood less than fourteen hands high. He was full of personality and I was smitten.

Once I acquired Manolito, Helena couldn't wait to own a horse too. Her parents had the funding to import a special horse for her from Poland. Paradox was a stunning, regal gelding who stood several hands higher than my short pony. Jealousy enveloped me when I first saw him. But my envy turned to elation when Manolito continued to win races against Paradox in the farm fields. He was extremely quick for a chubby pony; his determination trumped Paradox's size almost every race.

Helena and I continued to ride together every weekend. We'd arrive at the barn upon sunrise, saddle up as quickly as possible, and venture deep into the forest for late into sunset rides. On days that we'd wandered off too deep into the woods and couldn't find our way out, we'd give the horses long reins so they could guide us back safely to the stable, because they always found their way. As we gained confidence in our abilities, we formed our own (novice) junior riding school. We enthusiastically posted handmade ads throughout the village, inviting local children to learn from us. To our amazement, several students signed up. For a summer of Saturdays, we taught them how to mount, ride, groom, tack up, and clean the horses. I had no time for much else aside from that stable life that gave me purpose.

Monika

My parents moved us to another part of town the year following my season at the farm. I'd moved so much in my short life that every time I had to enroll in a different school, I was nervous. Fortunately one of the girls from our neighborhood moved at the same time as my family and we were assigned to the same class. I was relieved to begin High School with an acquaintance.

There were some students in my class that I thought of as 'The Religious Ones'. They behaved differently than my other classmates. Their zealousness polarized the class and I struggled to relate to them, thinking it awkward when any of them pursued a friendship with me. One by one they'd invite me to attend church. I'd always decline. None of them seemed to understand that I did not *need their God,* and I most certainly didn't want to go to church or be part of their group. Besides, my life was so full without knowing religion. I wondered why didn't they understand that? However, there was one girl in class who caused me to reconsider what I declared.

Monika was more authentic and relatable than I thought a Christian girl could be. Everyone in class liked her. She was always happy, telling jokes; making us laugh. Her genuine faith intrigued me, piquing my curiosity. She presented the idea of a loving God like my Scout Troop leaders had. I soon realized that Monika had something I didn't. As a young teen, I was beginning to overcome my childhood fears and anxieties, yet I felt empty of the joy she exuded. Occasionally she'd invite me to church with her to which I customarily replied, "No thanks". But I did become friends with her. Whenever she'd talk about her faith in God, I listened. Hearing about Jesus again gave me a sense of peace. I began to feel that God was waiting for me—summoning me. I began to consider that maybe it was *my* turn to take a step towards knowing Him. I wrestled with the thought and then tossed sentiment aside with the presumption that I could wait awhile.

A newspaper reporter came to visit our public school to interview local teens preparing for Christian theology class. He approached me in the midst of my gathered (school) friends during class break inquiring, "What about you? Will you also be confirmed (at the Church of Sweden)?" Trying to act composed in front of the other students, and unwilling to admit to the reporter whether I believed in God or not, I replied without hesitation, "No! I don't even believe in God!" Instinctively I knew my reaction was wrong. I had the revelation then that I did believe, but was convinced my life would be dull if I chose to become a Christian. I refused to relinquish what I considered 'fun' and didn't regard faith in God any further until later one freezing winter day when a horrendous tragedy impacted our family.

A Winter Day

We were home when my parents received a phone call from my mother's dearest friend, a sweet Christian lady who was a single mother of two boys. She rang to share the horrific news that one of her son's had just died after he was hit by a train in our hometown. He was only fifteen years old. We were stunned. It was a severe shock for our family. Soon after the accident my mom's friend came to visit us. I was dreading her arrival, wondering what could possibly be said to comfort her. How could I encourage her when I was so distraught by the loss myself? While my family paced the house waiting, I took Oscar outside to go to the bathroom.

My exhaled breath lingered in the gray silent air, as I stood alone in the freezing cold waiting for Oscar to relieve himself. The first snow of the season began to fall. During that still, vivid moment—she arrived. I froze with hesitation. *What should I say?* But the most amazing thing happened. We embraced. We cried. Then she held me for a long time. I felt the pain I saw in her eyes, yet there in the midst of our silent sadness, she exuded a grounded peace—an undeniable calm. Her face seemed to glow with light. I was perplexed. We didn't exchange words. None were needed. I pondered the reality that she had just lost her precious child yet she was comforting me instead of me comforting her! How could she have so much peace in the midst of such tragedy? That was an impactful moment.

My Scout Troop leaders, classmate Monika, and mother's friend were wonderful examples of the Jesus I had heard about in my youth. Love, peace, and kindness were evident through each of them so authentically. It was evident to me they had contentment that I did not. Getting to know them tenderized my heart to consider accepting the Gospel of Christ as truth. However, again I delayed a commitment to anything but the life path I had created for myself, basically just hanging out with friends to party.

My weekends were all about cruising up and down main street where my friends and I sought out older guys to purchase alcohol for us, go to local rock clubs like the Stopet to watch the latest band, or cruise by boat to one of the many Lake Sommen islands for nighttime soirees. I enjoyed what I thought was a good life, astonished that none of my friends or I never drowned after nighttime Island partying.

My parents' desire to have a child together finally came true. When my little brother Petter was born, we were all overjoyed; our family was complete. Yet I felt an increasing restlessness that I wasn't able to identify and the vice grip of loneliness began to pinch my heart once again. Then another day came when more seeds of faith in God were planted.

Leather Jacket

When I'd grown too tall to ride him, I sold Manolito and bought a larger horse named Nut Brown. But Nut Brown and I weren't a good match, so my desire to ride everyday began to fade. It was more interesting to stay out late partying with friends or listening to music. Boys began to notice me when my cousin Johan and I went out together. I welcomed the flattering attention they gave me, much more than horses, and they began to engage my curiosity over everything else.

Several of the guys in town, including Johan, had motorcycles. I was sixteen years old and opted for any thrilling opportunity to hitch a ride on the back of one of their bikes. The excitement of speeding through the open wind gave me a sense of freedom from life's daily bounds. I decided I wanted my own motorcycle. My friend Eva and I took lessons together, studying hard to achieve the goal of gaining a motorcycle license. The Swedish training course was a long, difficult one. It took us about nine months, but we celebrated when we passed the rigorous test by purchasing our own Yamaha 125cc motorcycles. My passion for riding had turned from horses to motorbikes. Eva and I became proficient bikers who rode together regularly. Sometimes we were even 'allowed' to join our guy friend's rides. It was exhilarating!

It was on one of those rides that I experienced my first miracle. One of the guys invited me to take a ride with him on his big chopper. Before we headed out for an evening highway ride I stopped by home to grab my helmet and questioned whether I should wear denim or leather jacket. I opted for leather since he was wearing his. We sped off, but didn't get very far out of town when a car swerved over to our side of the road. To avoid being hit by oncoming cars, my friend had no choice but to go straight over a small hillside into a deep ditch. I flew off the bike through the ditch, and then back up the hill across the two-lane highway flying on my stomach onto into highway traffic headed both directions. My friend hung on to his bike for dear life, ramping up unto the highway sliding behind me, under the chopper! We both finally came to a stop, miraculously without getting struck by oncoming cars.

An ambulance arrived quickly to take us to the hospital. My friend needed some stitches. The skin on both of my hands had been scraped off, my helmet was crushed around my chin, and my jacket destroyed. But the entire front side of my body was completely protected because I had chosen the leather jacket! We basically walked away from the accident with mostly scrapes and bruising, but I knew our lives were spared that night. I then began to ponder the existence of God again.

London 'Punks'

During High School I met Håkan. I had crushes on a lot of boys, but he was the first love since my childhood romance with Mikael. We were inseparable for about six months until he ended our relationship a year after the motorcycle accident. I suffered the rejection with shock. The pain of loss I'd experienced throughout my childhood culminated in so much heartache that I decided I must leave our small town for a change of environment to help me process everything. I was still struggling with learning issues and didn't see the need to finish my final year of Gymnasiet (Junior College). After much persuasion, my parents allowed me to quit school early to join my friends Marianne and Eva, who were working as Au Pairs in London.

My friend Romy and I left for London together. We rode by commercial truck to Belgium and then cruised on a twenty-four hour ocean ferry ride to Dover, England. We settled into our small cabin for the night sleep not realizing the North Sea to be one of the worst places to travel during winter. A huge storm that violently rolled the ferry, like a toy boat in splashing bath water, woke us up in the middle of the night. Seasickness overwhelmed me. I trembled as I crawled on all fours to the cabin bathroom where I began vomiting throughout the night, convinced we were going to capsize and drown. I couldn't stop crying, reminiscing about Håkan and my family—missing them more than ever before and afraid I would never see them again.

When morning came, I was relieved that we'd made it across safely to the Dover, England port.

We met up with Marianne and Eva who encouraged Romy and me to seek jobs in the Southgate area of London. The first family I was hired by lived in a traditional English Row house. The father, son, and I did not get along well, though the mother had a pleasing personality. They were upper middle class hosts who hired Au Pairs to help improve their social status in addition to fulfilling housekeeping needs. As a result they often worked me harder than it was necessary. My duties were to care for their son, clean the house, and iron the father's shirts each day. They were obsessive with cleanliness and I was perplexed—why did one man have so many shirts that needed ironing every day and why did the mother need her chrome bath taps (faucets) kept sparkling throughout the day? It was tiring work for seven pounds a week wage.

Eva earned twelve pounds a week, more than any of us. I envied her income. While our host families provided room and board, our cash wages barely covered other expenses. We learned to survive though, finding a way to continuously party for the two days off we had weekly. We formed friendships with a group of fifteen other Swedish Au Pairs working in London, attracting the attention of British guys who sought us out wherever we went. We got drunk together in the Underground (subway) bathrooms, where six to eight of us crammed in together at one time to pass around one cheap bottle of alcohol we'd share in lieu of spending money at a costly Pub. We'd strut through London's West End—bustling Piccadilly Circus, and Royal St. James's Park dressed like 'Punk' rockers in strange mismatched clothes and bright colored hair. We'd then continue our brewed binges at famous rock clubs like the Marquee, Dingwalls, and the Music Machine, where we saw many emerging bands play—Blondie, The Police, Cheap Trick, Dire Straights, and The Steve Gibbons band.

We weren't exactly promiscuous girls, but sometimes we got into trouble. We often stayed out later than the last London Underground (subway) train ran and lacking money for a cab, incautiously hitchhiked home with strangers. We suffered a few late night mishaps, but were miraculously protected from calamity.

Four families hired me over the course of six months I lived in London. I barely lasted one month with the first family before they fired me. I also was fired from the second family, and then I quit the final two. Working as an Au Pair didn't turn out well. Though I worked hard, I wasn't exactly an employer's commodity, as a seventeen year-old who considered partying with friends more inspiring than house and childcare chores.

My inherent loneliness dissipated in London somewhat, but I was feeling vulnerable and homesick so far from my family. By mid 1977, Marianne, Romy, Eva, and I all agreed our London venture was over, reluctantly returning to our uneventful hometown. For our boat cruise from London to Gothenburg, we changed clothes to appear like the punkers we thought we were for our *grand* return. As the bus from Gothenburg pulled into Tranås, my heart sank into a chasm of displeasure because the town appeared smaller than I'd remembered.

Our parents were at the bus station waiting for us. Their celebration unanimously turned to dismay when our costumed attire upstaged our entrance. My mother sternly informed me I would not be allowed to set foot into the kitchen where she had prepared a fine dinner until I *"washed off all my crud"* (makeup). Bo didn't know what to say. My friend Marianne's parents were so concerned by the site of her, that they covered her in a blanket and brought her home through their garage concealed from her elderly grandparents. Our 'Punk' personas were quenched by parental disapproval, but the town news editor caught word of our London adventure and published a favorable front-page article in the local paper about us "Here They Are…Home Again!"

City of Angels

Following my London journey, I was on a quest to explore more than what Tranås had to offer, so I accepted full-time work at a local factory in an effort to save enough money to travel again. I'd had a long-term desire to visit my birth country so I determined southern California to be my next destination. Another group of local girls had left Sweden for nanny employment abroad and invited me to join them. They were living north of Los Angeles in Malibu, working as well paid Au Pairs, who were given cars to drive to support their child-care responsibilities. I was happy to hear that house cleaning wasn't generally required because most of the host families hired housekeepers. The opportunity to work under those circumstances seemed too good to pass up. I packed my bags, left behind a new boyfriend, whom I'd grown deeply in love with, and flew to the City of Angels with my close friend Pia.

As we began the descent on our flight to LAX, we peered out the airplane window, awed by the beauty we saw everywhere beyond the massive urban concrete sprawl. The miles of long sand strands laced with sky-high palm trees that bordered deep blue Pacific waters took our breath away. The landscape was quite different than what we'd imagined.

Our Swedish friend Lotta, picked us up at the airport in a big brown Suburban, the biggest car I'd ever seen. As we departed the airport and merged into hectic traffic, I thought to myself, *I don't know if I'll ever be able to drive a car in this city!* We rode through

Marina Del Rey, passed by the historical Santa Monica fishing pier where I saw what looked like a miniature castle housing a carousel, and up Pacific Coast Highway north to the Malibu shore where we saw dozens of wet suited surfers catching ocean waves. It was a surreal drive on a perfect sunny day.

My first Au Pair assignment was to take over Lotta's position with a Malibu family. When I arrived to replace her, I wasn't well received. They loved Lotta who had developed a close relationship with their daughter and her role was hard to fill. The family and I made an effort to work together, but it didn't pan out, and I had to move two weeks later.

The family Pia worked for graciously allowed me to stay with them at their hillside ocean view home until I found a new job. I helped her clean the house— which was in severe disorder, take care of their five-year old son and friendly flea-infested sheepdog. We'd swim with them in the pool and spend days with them at Zuma beach. It was a fabulous location to live.

I enjoyed my time off visiting different beaches, dancing at 'The Sun Spot', a popular disco in Santa Monica near the coast Highway, and late night Hollywood clubbing with my dear friends Milada, Lotta, Mona, and Pia.

One evening I was invited to an event that initiated a major turning point in my life. Milada had plans to go with her boyfriend, Domenique—a French Fashion photographer—to a birthday party in Beverly Hills for Grammy recording artist, Donna Summer. She couldn't go because she had the flu and asked me if I'd like to take her place. "I'm sorry you're sick Milada, but I'd *love* to!" At nineteen years old I was elated by the opportunity to meet the Queen of 70's Disco. Dominique introduced me to Ms. Summer soon after we arrived. She was very friendly and we chatted a bit. I was happy to hear about her experiences in Sweden on a music tour and about how she loved spending time in Stockholm.

Then Dominique introduced me to Elvis Presley's ex-wife and her fashion model boyfriend. While I stood there with the three of them, attempting to be a part of the conversation, Ms. Presley's boyfriend asked if I was also a model signed with the Nina Blanchard modeling agency—one of the most high profile agencies in Los Angeles. I informed him "No...I'm not". He thought I ought to meet with the Agency. I didn't take his encouragement seriously until Dominique made an effort to convince me I was model material and then offered to personally set up an interview for me with Ms. Blanchard. I was somewhat intimidated by the idea, but excited at the potential and decided to consider it.

During our car ride back to Malibu later that evening, Dominique coached me "Even though you are thin Titania, you will need to lose some weight to become a successful model. Take the time you need to get prepared to meet Nina." That motivated me to want to lose the necessary weight. I thought if I returned to Sweden sooner than planned it might be easier. I was missing my boyfriend and was eager to see him again.

Before I returned home to Europe, my good friend Kris, who knew I'd never met my biological father, convinced me to attempt to find him. Though reluctant, I finally acquiesced to her relentless nudging. I knew my father's name so I was able to locate an associated address in Los Angeles through the local Police department. Kris drove me there and stood on the front door stoop with me as we arrived unannounced to ring the doorbell. I held my breath. I began to sweat as my heart pounded with apprehension. An elderly woman answered the door. Her eyes widened with surprise. Though we'd never met, my father's mother knew immediately who I was. It was an awkward pause.

She invited us inside where she made a phone call to my father. Anxiety overwhelmed me. As a child I used to imagine myself sitting up in a tree looking down and waiting for him to walk by—just to catch a glimpse of what he looked like. Kris and I followed his mother in her big Cadillac to my father's apartment so we could meet. When I first saw him, I was paralyzed with conflicting emotions. I didn't know how to relate to him. I'd never seen a photo of him and didn't know what to expect. I was surprised by his unfamiliarity. We didn't resemble each other at all. He was receptive to me, but we struggled to connect. I think he was in shock as well. The moments we spent together were mutually difficult. I left that evening knowing I didn't want a relationship with him or his family. It was simply too painful for me. My father pursued me, and we spoke on the phone a few times while I was still in California. With every conversation more emotional challenges cramped my comfort, so once I returned to Sweden, we lost touch. He wrote me a letter a few years later to let me know he had cancer, but I didn't respond and never saw him again.

Battling Bulimia

The comfort of home usually filled my heart with rest, but my next trip to Tranås only offered more heartache. My boyfriend and I broke up soon after I arrived in Sweden since we had grown apart during my stay in California. Making a quick turnaround, I headed back to Los Angeles sooner than planned.

I quit Au Pair work and moved from Malibu to the active community of Manhattan Beach to live with new friends Beth and Kim. We lived in an apartment a block from the ocean where we watched volleyball tournaments, hung out with local surfers, and jogged on the boardwalk. I loved running along the beach where I could smell the salt water and hear the sound of waves rolling against the shore. We had a great time living together. I enrolled in acting classes at Santa Monica City College and I had managed to lose a decent amount of weight in prep for my meeting with the modeling agency.

Without a car yet, I needed to find a job close to the apartment. The Good Earth restaurant had an opening and their menu was fairly healthy. I liked the staff, but it wasn't the best environment to fight cravings for a girl who needed to stay thin. I found it a challenge to keep off the pounds I had lost. I continued to gain more and more weight, perpetually postponing my meeting with the Blanchard Agency. I became discouraged to the point that I was losing hope for the one great opportunity that had been offered me. My chronic childhood anxiety resumed, as the grasp on the future I had a vision for, was slowly slipping away. It may have been triggered by fear of success, fear of failing, or both, but my soul was unsettled.

My confidence decreased with each pound gained, yet I channeled my insecurity through food consumption. On one of my work shifts, the restaurant chef, who I had a bit of an infatuation with, blurted out "Oh Titania, you are a very big woman!" as I walked into his kitchen. Despair turned to despondency when such a discouraging comment came from a guy I was attracted to. So I began to eat more and more and then purge myself by vomiting after I ate. I couldn't allow myself more poundage from excess calories—but I *needed* the food for comfort.

Lotta took me out for coffee one night and after hearing me vent about my challenges, she said, "Titania you are obsessed with food! All you talk about is food and your weight battles." I wouldn't hear what she had to say. Her perception didn't resonate with me as truth then. Even though I purged after every meal, I was in a grave denial. It was my well-kept secret—*no one* knew about my issue. After about one year attempting to lose the weight unsuccessfully, I decided to give up on the idea of modeling and return again to Sweden. I thought a few months at home would offer some fresh perspective.

As I settled in on the plane flight back to Europe, the flight attendant handed me a magazine to read that just happened to contain an article about a young girl who suffered with Bulimia. As I read about her illness, I began to realize that I was Bulimic! The blinders of denial fell off and I felt the sharp pain of my ill reality. I panicked, *Oh my God, Bulimia is defining me!* I had the classic symptoms and could no longer avoid the glaring truth. I didn't realize how badly my health had deteriorated. Then I heard Lotta's comments playback in mind, and I was scared.

Some balance returned to life on my visit back home. Seeing my parents, my brother, and my aged little Oscar helped me to feel better. I spent time with friends, took long walks in the woods, and rode horses as much as I could. My Bulimia battle subsided a little bit in Sweden. Though my weight was still a concern, my eating habits improved and I vomited less. However, I had lost trust and confidence in myself. I was navigating towards health without a compass. I needed a mentor and didn't know where I could find help. I had planned to stay in Sweden for about two months before I returned to California with hope to pursue the dream of modeling again. But I was traumatized with shattered self-trust. I wondered *what could prevent me from falling back into this horrible habit and lifestyle again? Could I regain self-trust and do right the next time?*

I had a return ticket for three months away. The closer it got to my return date, the more anxious and fearful I became. I was borderline frantic. I sought advice from my parents and dearest friends. *Should I stay home or should I return to America and continue to pursue my dream?* Conflicting advice ensued. Some of my friends thought I ought to stay in Sweden and some thought I should to go back to Malibu and not give up. Lack of clear direction was disorienting. But without the courage to tell anyone about my Bulimic disorder, none of the advice I received gave me clarity. So I kept a terrible dark secret that scared me so much, hidden from those who loved me. I realized that for the first time in my life, there was no one who could help me, even though they were willing to listen.

Time Stopped

On an evening, ten days before my scheduled flight, I went downstairs from my bedroom to the kitchen in an effort to seek advice from my mother just one more time. She was sitting at the kitchen table reading a book with her back toward me, unaware I had entered the room feeling lost and desperate. With tears falling down my cheeks, I looked at the kitchen clock; it was 10:13pm. That moment I heard a supernatural voice for the first time. I looked up as it sounded like it came from above me. It was the most deep, calm, and loving voice that I had ever heard—like that of a man, but sort of heavenly. Though I was in Sweden, I heard his words spoken to me in English—catching me off guard, "She cannot help you, as you have already tried."

In that moment I simply turned around as if I was being guided, back up the stairs into my bedroom. I closed the door, turned off the lights, lit a candle on my night table, and got down on my knees. I took a deep breath and looked up, as if up to heaven exclaiming "I do not know if you exist God, but if you do, I need help!" I had never prayed to God before. My eyes still flooded with quiet tears while internally my emotions rolled relentlessly like huge waves pounding, crashing, against the shore; the opposite of calm. I had no peace. I bowed my head and prayed the most desperate prayer of my young adult life. The same calming voice spoke to me again, "You can go back to Los Angeles, and I will always take care of you". It was a magnificent moment where I felt the most supernatural peace I'd ever experienced.

I then crawled on my hands and knees back across the floor into my bed and pulled the covers over me very carefully to not make any sudden moves so the peaceful presence would linger. The last words I whispered that night were "Oh please God, don't let this be gone in the morning. Let me keep this feeling forever."

The next morning when I woke up, His presence was still with me. I felt like a new person with a grounded internal strength. All my fear and anxiety had been replaced with joy. I was confident that I would be taken care of in Los Angeles. For the first time in my life I felt peace that gave me courage. That night I recovered from Bulimia and never had the urge to purge ever again. God had healed me. That was the second miracle in my life.

I couldn't wait to share the news about what had happened the night before with all of my friends and family. *I had prayed to God and He had answered me!* I don't know if anyone completely understood my experience, but I believe the change in my countenance was evident. My anxiety was gone and I was confident about my returning again to Los Angeles.

The Third Miracle

I returned to California as a twenty-three year old with refreshed purpose. It was almost Christmas when I had moved in with another friend, Joyce, who had a one-bedroom apartment in the heart of Santa Monica, six blocks from the beach. Coming back felt different. The idea of becoming a model now seemed less important to me. My desire to find out more about the God whose voice I'd heard back in Sweden became my quest. I could feel His comforting presence and I no longer felt alone even when I was by myself. I was intrigued by His love for me. I didn't have an idea what to do next but I pursued him every day asking, "Lord, I know now that you are real, but what about Jesus? How and where does he fit in? I want to know more about him".

Close by our apartment near 7th and California Street, was the historic St. Monica Catholic Church. In awe of the elegant 1920's architecture, I found myself drawn there whenever I walked by. I'd often go sit inside, when the building was empty, just to pray. I felt close to God while I was there. During one of my many visits, I met Monsignor O'Flaherty, a very gentle 80 year-old priest who became my mentor. We began to meet weekly in his office next door to the church. He helped me learn more about my newly found faith. I then began asking God persistently for the next three months, *"Who is Jesus?"* I had to know.

Then one day a third miracle happened.

I had gone into the church early to wait for my appointment with the Monsignor. I enjoyed the peace I felt in the sanctuary while waiting for my meeting. On the ceiling above the sanctuary altar was a breathtaking life size gold painting of Jesus Christ, the Son of God. His arms were stretched out wide and his eyes beautifully painted. The art seemed to glow. That day I noticed there was only one person in the church. She was close to the altar, sitting on the left side of the aisle. I was sitting several rows behind her near the rear of the sanctuary. As I kneeled down to pray I glanced up at the painting of Jesus, as I always did whenever I visited. It was quiet. All of a sudden the painted eyes seemed to come alive! I blinked hard, looking again and again. I wasn't really seeing what I saw...was I? But his eyes came alive! Then a thin white beam of filtered light slowly emerged from the painting and descended down to the floor in front of the altar. The white light then gently evolved into a radiant gold shape of a body. As I stared in disbelief, Jesus Christ then appeared standing in front of the altar!

I remained kneeling where I was and then again heard the same voice of God that I'd heard in my bedroom in Sweden a few months previously...."This IS Jesus Christ, the same Jesus Christ, who walked the earth nearly 2000 years ago, is now walking up to you, and you do not even have to go to him!" As I heard His voice, I watched Jesus walk down the aisle toward me as if in slow motion straight through the wooden pews! What I saw was so unbelievable.

My mind was racing with many thoughts...*I'm Titania Lindfors from* Tranås *Sweden and it's 1984, how could this be happening?* In spite of my awed reaction, I felt the peace of God surround me to calm my mind. Spontaneous tears flowed down my cheeks. I knew it was all really happening.

I don't know how long it took for all that transpired. It was a captivating moment that happened in a timeless manner. Then suddenly, Jesus was standing right in front of me! His magnificent Holiness and power resonated from Him. His robe looked like it had been spun from gold. There are no words to accurately express the magnitude of the supernatural manifestation. My initial thought was *He is so big.* The feeling I had in His presence was like nothing I'd felt before. I was overwhelmed. In that moment I knew with everything in me, that no one would be able to deny that He is God, and that every person on the earth would have to bow to Him. His tremendous Spirit immobilized me and I was unable to move any part of my body but my eyes. I kept still.

My head was level with his stomach. My heart raced as I thought, *He is the very Jesus whom I had been asking God about so persistently for several months, who was now standing in front of me. He had walked up to me, FROM OUT OF A PAINTING!* He then lifted His arms up around me; very slowly, which gave me a moment to fully receive the miracle that was taking place. He held me for a while. I do not know for how long. Then He spoke, and said to me, "I will always take care of you."

The radiant glory exuded from Him, making my body weak. My spirit and soul bore witness to who He was. Feeling unworthy of His love, I became acutely aware of my imperfections, and my humanity. I knew I was the opposite of holy. I understood in that moment why we all need His forgiveness and redemption. I had an immediate revelation of why He died on the cross and was resurrected for all people. After some time had passed, He said, "It is time to go now". I was still unable to move myself, so He lifted me up onto my feet and steadied me. My tears were unstoppable, in reaction to His Divineness.

During that moment I became aware of the lady near the front of the church. I noticed that she had turned her head and was watching me. I think she could see that something extraordinary was happening, though I don't know if she was able to see Him.

Jesus then began to escort me out of the Sanctuary; it was time for my appointment next door. My legs were very weak, and though I wanted nothing more than to turn my head to look at him, I was unable to. Then I felt Him slowly fade away, and by the time I stepped out of the front door of the church, He was gone.

Monsignor O'Flaherty came downstairs to greet me and found me sitting in his waiting room. I had lost my speech and was still unable to talk. Tears continued to stream down my face. The Monsignor then helped me gently up from the couch and walked me into his office. He sat me down in one of his two chairs, while he sat down in the other. Then he quietly waited for me to regain my speech. My body was limp and I still felt very weak. When I was finally able to speak again about forty-five minutes later, it took immense effort for me to accurately share what I had just experienced. My English words did not seem adequate enough to describe Jesus, nor capture His Holiness. It almost felt like I was speaking with mud coming out of my mouth. I fought to find the proper words to describe the Divine encounter. I was concerned that I might dishonor Jesus by using such plain language. Yet I was so empowered by what had happened. After a while the Monsignor tenderly asked me if I realized how I was truly honored and blessed to have experienced such a miracle? I said, yes I think I did. But then questioned, "Why was I chosen to have Jesus Christ appear to me?" It was too much for me to completely grasp. *Why me?*

Then I heard God speak to my heart and say, "I want you to share your story with anyone who will listen."

Epilogue

It has now been more than twenty-six years since I had a personal visitation from Jesus Christ. I am forever grateful for the encounter at an early age, giving me the chance to know Him most of my adult life. I would not change that for anything.

Though my life has not always been easy or pain free, Jesus has always been with me. He is my provider, protector, friend and so much more.

He is faithful.

**You will find Me
when you seek Me
with all your heart.**

(Jeremiah 29:13)

With my mother in America

Uncle Hasse

Småland (Sweden)

Celebrating my birthday in Sweden with my cousins.

Swedish Dagmamma (Daycare) Eva and me with an unknown boy.

A playmate and my cousin Agnetha at our new apartment complex

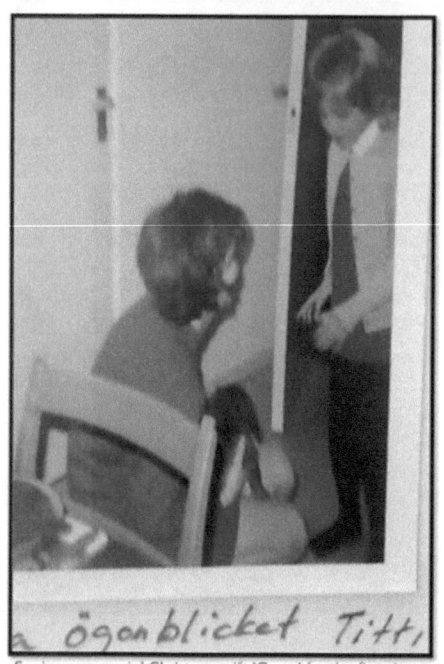

a ögonblicket Titti

Seeing my special Christmas gift 'Oscar' for the first time.

n av många, många turer
ed O. i cykelkorgen.

With Oscar

With Mother and Bo

My pony Manolito at the farm

Eva and me on our Yahama's.

Titti Lindfors

— Jag ska inte konfirmera mig. Varför ska man göra det? Det är inget kul att gå i kyrkan, bara jobbigt. Jag hinner inte för jag rider.

Man har ingen nytta av att konfirmeras. De flesta gör det för att få presenter. Det är ju meningen att man ska göra det för att man tror på Gud. Jag har fått välja själv.

Nä, jag tror inte precis på Gud.

News article stating my denial of faith in God.

At the Marquee in London with Eva and Marianne

pade som au-pair i London

Nu väntar skolan igen för Marianne Widmalm, som stannade hemma åtta månader i England.

Det är spännande att resa utomlands och pröva något nytt, tycker Eva Bridgeman. I Tranås kan man ju inte gå och dra ...

Drömresan till USA hägrar för Romy Palmqvist.

Titti Lindfors tentade in i Enfield Chase school i London, och pluggade engelska. Det var lätt att komma in och överlag för svenskarna ett gott betyg i engelska språket.

Interviewed at Hollywood KROQ radio station with Swedish friends

Seeing the Santa Monica Pier in California for the first time

At a Hollywood party

St. Monica Catholic Church Sanctuary

www.ingramcontent.com/pod-product-compliance
Lightning Source LLC
Chambersburg PA
CBHW030525290526
45786CB00004B/1622